شكرا
SHUKRAN

Dedicated to Joan Evans

Our neighbour, friend, and family.

Shukran for your kindness, laughter, and the love you shared.

You will always hold a special place in our hearts.

Rest in peace.

With love,

Albert, Maha, Lena, and Edward Shammas

My Heart Says SHUKRAN

Words by Edward Shammas

Art by Mayssa Kennouche

"**Shukran**"
means thank you in Arabic.
We say Shukran for all the
gifts in our lives.

Shukran

Shukran family,
love I see

Shukran
home,
safe for me.

Kareem

Shukran **food**, yum, yum, yum

Shukran **sun,** warm and fun.

Shukran clouds,
crying sky

Shukran **sea**, fish swim by.

Shukran
tree,
dates soo sweet

Shukran
cat,
kind and neat.

TOYS

YUMMY
Arabic
SOUNDS
Arabic Alphabet
Arab Role Models

Shukran Grandpa and Grandma, too

Shukran all,
I love you!

Family

عائلة

Aaila

Home

بيت

Bayt

Food

أكل

Akel

Sun

شمس

Shams

Sea

بحر

Bahr

Tree

شجرة

Shajara

Cat

قطة

Qiṭṭa

Grandma

جدة

Jida

Grandpa

جدو

Jidou

Clouds

غيوم

Ghuyoom

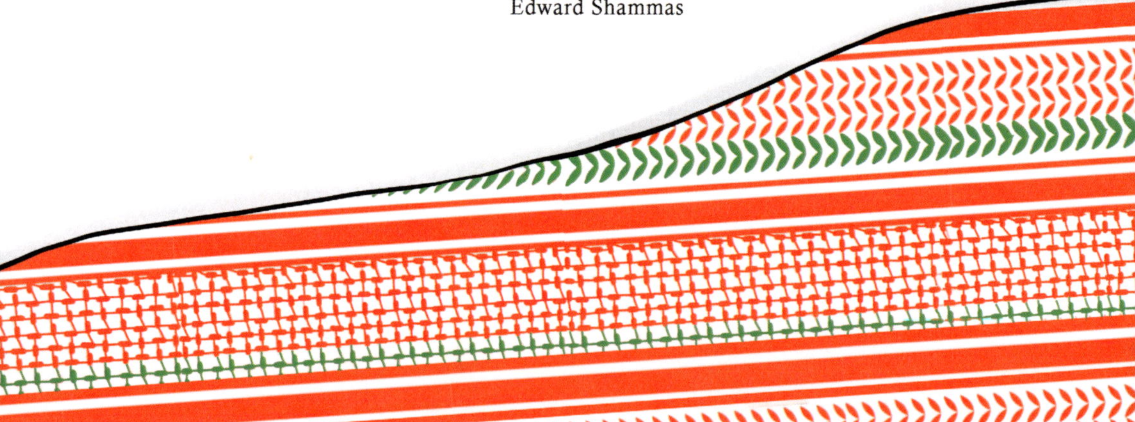